TODAY'S GREAT
QUARTERBACKS

JOE FLACCO

By Ryan Nagelhout

Gareth Stevens
Publishing

RIGHT ON!

Please visit our website www.garethstevens.com. For a free color catalog of all our high-quality books, call toll free 1-800-542-2595 or fax 1-877-542-2596.

Library of Congress Cataloging-in-Publication Data

Nagelhout, Ryan.
Joe Flacco / by Ryan Nagelhout.
 p. cm. — (Today's great quarterbacks)
Includes index.
ISBN 978-1-4824-0145-5 (pbk.)
ISBN 978-1-4824-0146-2 (6-pack)
ISBN 978-1-4824-0143-1 (library binding)
1. Flacco, Joe — Juvenile literature. 2. Football players — United States — Biography — Juvenile literature. 3. Quarterbacks (Football) — United States — Biography — Juvenile literature. I. Nagelhout, Ryan. II. Title.
GV939.F555 N34 2014
796.332092—dc23

First Edition

Published in 2014 by
Gareth Stevens Publishing
111 East 14th Street, Suite 349
New York, NY 10003

Copyright © 2014 Gareth Stevens Publishing

Designer: Nicholas Domiano
Editor: Ryan Nagelhout

Photo credits: Cover, p. 1 David Dermer/Diamond Images/Getty Images; p. 5 Michael Locciano/Getty Images Entertainment/Getty Images; p. 7 Mike Ehrmann/Getty Images Sport/Getty Images; p. 9 Al Bello/Getty Images Sport/Getty Images; p. 11 Jon Kopaloff/FilmMagic/Getty Images; p. 13 Keith Srakocic/AP Photos; p. 15 Simon Bruty/Sports Illustrated/Getty Images; p. 17 Jeff Fusco/Getty Images Sport/Getty Images; p. 19 Chris McGrath/Getty Images Sport/Getty Images; p. 21 Doug Kapustin/MCT/Getty Images; p. 23 Cindy Ord/Getty Images Entertainment/Getty Images; p. 25 Timothy A. Clary/AFP/Getty Images; p. 27 Steve Ruark/AP Photos; p. 29 Alberto E. Rodriguez/Getty Images Entertainment/Getty Images;

Printed in the United States of America

CPSIA compliance information: Batch #CW14GS: For further information contact Gareth Stevens, New York, New York at 1-800-542-2595.

CONTENTS

Meet Joe

Joe Flacco is a **champion** quarterback.

He plays in the National Football

League (NFL).

Joe was born on January 16, 1985, in Audubon, New Jersey. His parents are Karen and Steve Flacco.

The Sporting Life

Joe loved sports growing up. He played football and baseball with his brothers and sister.

In 1999, Joe started at quarterback for the Audubon Green Wave football team. He played 3 years in high school.

11

Joe went to **college** at the University of Pittsburgh for 2 years. He didn't get to play much football, though. In 2005, he went to play at the University of Delaware.

Blue Bomber

In 2006, Joe started at quarterback for Delaware. He set 20 school records in two seasons with the Fightin' Blue Hens! He did big things at such a small school.

NFL teams liked Joe's skills. The Baltimore Ravens picked him 18th overall in the 2008 NFL **Draft**.

17

Playoff Performer

Joe started for the Ravens in 2008. He was the first **rookie** quarterback to win two playoff games. He won a rookie of the year award!

Joe quickly became one of the best

quarterbacks in Ravens history.

He leads the team in career yards,

touchdown passes, **completions**,

and attempts.

On June 25, 2011, Joe got married.

He and his wife, Dana, have two

children.

Super Ravens

In 2013, Joe led the Ravens to a
win in Super Bowl 47. He beat the
San Francisco 49ers, 34-31. Joe was
named the game's Most Valuable
Player (MVP)!

Joe loves to help others. He works with the Special Olympics and many charities in Baltimore.

What's Next?

Joe's career is just taking off.

What will he accomplish next?

Timeline

1985   Joe is born on January 16.

1999   Joe plays quarterback for Audubon High School.

2003   Joe goes to the University of Pittsburgh.

2005   Joe moves to the University of Delaware.

2008   Baltimore Ravens pick Joe 18th overall in the NFL Draft.

2009   Joe becomes the first rookie quarterback in NFL history to win two playoff games.

2013   Ravens win Super Bowl 47. Joe wins MVP.

Books

Krumenauer, Heidi. *Joe Flacco*. Hockessin, DE: Mitchell Lane Publishers, 2010.

Sandler, Michael. *Joe Flacco and the Baltimore Ravens: Super Bowl XLVII*. New York, NY: Bearport Publishing, 2014.

Websites

Joe Flacco's Official Site

joeflacco5.com
Find out what Joe does on and off the field.

Joe Flacco's Stats

http://www.nfl.com/player/joeflacco/382/profile
Check out Joe's stats and download his biography on his official NFL player page.

Publisher's note to educators and parents: Our editors have carefully reviewed these websites to ensure that they are suitable for students. Many websites change frequently, however, and we cannot guarantee that a site's future contents will continue to meet our high standards of quality and educational value. Be advised that students should be closely supervised whenever they access the Internet.

Glossary

champion: the overall winner

college: a school after high school

completions: a successful pass in football

draft: a way to pick new football players for the NFL

rookie: a first-year player in pro sports

Index